The Lifetime of Torah Library

TALMUD
WITH TRAINING WHEELS

**With a foreword
by Rabbi Adin Steinsaltz**

An Absolute Beginner's Guide to Talmud

JOEL LURIE GRISHAVER

Table of Contents

1. The Day the Talmud Started 5

2. The Anatomy of the Talmud Page 12

3. From Ezra to the Mishnah 18

4. The Written Torah/The Oral Torah 23

5. From the Mishnah to the Gemara 28

6. Talmudic Tool Box 35

7. Epilogue: Using This Translation 43

8. Lexicon of Talmudic Vocabulary 45

Credits

Cover: *From Alef On*, 1995, Oil on Linen by Samuel Bak. Courtesy of Pucker Gallery, Boston.
Pages 5/8: © Hulton-Deutsch Collection/CORBIS ■ Page 6: © Historical Picture Archive/CORBIS
Page 11: © Jules Porter Photography ■ Page 15: © Erica Lanser ■ Page 19: Chris Heller/CORBIS
Page 20: © Walter Biblikow ■ Pages 22/25: © Archivo Iconografico, S.A./CORBIS ■ Pages 29/30/
31: © Bettmann/CORBIS ■ Page 44: © Ohr Torah Stone.

ISBN #1-891662-29-5

Copyright © 2003 Joel Lurie Grishaver

Torah Aura Productions• 4423 Fruitland Avenue, Los Angeles, CA 90058
(800) BE-TORAH • (800) 238-6724 • (323) 585-7312 • fax (323) 585-0327
Website WWW.TORAHAURA.COM

MANUFACTURED IN CHINA

Foreword

History shows that no Jewish community anywhere in the world has survived without the Talmud. In those communities where Talmud study was seen as a central focus of daily life, all aspects of Jewish life flourished and formed Jewish leadership, communal institutions and scholarship.

However, in those communities where Talmud study had somehow fallen away, the interwoven strands of the Jewish community themselves began to unravel, and some of the best of our people drifted elsewhere to seek out other challenging and rigorous disciplines.

It is for this reason that I welcome the renewed interest in Talmud study that is now becoming evident in the United States. Of course, each country needs instruments that fit its particular profile and culture. The Talmud study circles now springing up in the United States incorporate both an emphasis on Jewish unity and a respect for the high levels of secular education achieved by many American Jews. Similarly, this teaching guide on the English Talmud, which is especially designed for the American audience, uses teaching methods and figures that are already familiar to the reader.

As the seminal work of Jewish culture, religion and civilization, the Talmud both epitomizes our heritage and directs our future. May American Jewry thrive under its tutelage.

Adin Steinsaltz

Getting into the Talmud is no easy matter, even for those Jews who are ardent to recover for themselves what their ancestors once knew...for Talmudic learning is a collective. You do not "read" the Talmud, you "learn" it, preferably with a _haver_, or a fellow student, and always with a rabbi.... In the traditional yeshivah, the Talmud is not "learned" in a monotone. The Talmud is the music for a choir of voices; it is sung, and the music conveys the thrust and parry, the give and take of argument, which is what is truly Talmudic about the Talmud.

Jacob Neusner, from the Preface to *Invitation to Talmud*

The Talmud is not a schematic textbook, but essentially a slice of life. As such, it commences for no person at the beginning.

When a person begins to study Talmud, he always finds himself right in the middle of things, no matter where he starts.

Only through study and combination of facts can he arrive at the ability to understand what he has already studied; his comprehension grows constantly deeper as he peruses the material over and over again.

Adin Steinsaltz, *The Essential Talmud*, page 274

The Day the Talmud Started

If you want to understand the Talmud, you need to know the story of a single day (or perhaps a week*).

In 458 B.C.E. Ezra gathered the fragmented elements of Jewish community together by the Water Gate. There, in a ceremony of rededication, the Torah was read from beginning to end.

The Context

- In 586 B.C.E. the Babylonians destroyed the Temple, Jerusalem and the Land of Israel. Ten thousand Jews were carried away as exiles to the Land of Babylon.

- The prophet Jeremiah told these exiles, "Build houses and live in them. Plant gardens and eat their fruit. Take wives and husbands and have children, and take wives and husbands for your sons and daughters so that they can have children. Continue to multiply and do not shrink. Seek the peace of the city where I have sent you in exile and pray to the Eternal for its peace, because in the peace of that city you will find peace" (Jeremiah 29:5–7). Jeremiah also told the people that God would return them to the Land of Israel in seventy years.

- On cue, making that return possible, Persia, under king Cyrus, defeated Babylonia and became "top dog" in the region.

- In 538 B.C.E. Cyrus issued an edict giving permission for the Jews to go back to their homeland and rebuild their Temple. Some Jews went, but they couldn't get their act together. They laid the foundation for a new Temple but couldn't get it built. (You know about building funds!) They found themselves in the midst of lots of conflicts. There were conflicts between the rich and the poor. The Jewish community that came from Babylonia struggled with the population that stayed behind over the nature of authentic Judaism. There were problems with the ever-changing nature of Persian politics.

- In 515 B.C.E. a second Temple was finished, but the people were nowhere near being organized or unified.

* The history of this period is clouded. In the Book of Ezra we have the description of one gathering; in the Book of Nehemiah we have another. Academics argue about whether there were one or two, and which one came first. For us this does not matter; it is the power of the moment and the power of the memory that are significant.

Enter Ezra

Ezra was empowered by an edict from Artaxerexes, the latest Persian ruler, to go to the Land of Israel and use the king's authority to get the Jewish people together. He arrived, spent several months organizing and then held a gathering of renewal. The high point of this gathering was the public reading of the entire Torah.

Shemaryahu Talmon, an important Israeli biblical historian, **believes** that this was the first time that the Torah was ever brought out in public. Up to this moment it had been a priest's book, kept in the Temple, with the population having access only to the portions that were read aloud to them. This was when the Torah had her debutante ball.

Richard Elliot Freedman, a modern American biblical scholar, **believes** that this was the Torah's premiere party. The final document we know as the Torah had just been cobbled together (by Ezra) out of the various distinct holy documents (J, E, P, D, etc.), each used by a different segment of the Jewish people. This document and this reading unified Jews from Judea (J) and Jews from Israel (E); it brought together priests from the Shiloh faction (P1) and priests from the family of Tzadok (P2). The document itself expressed the new beginning of this moment. (D) is a different story.

Said Cyrus, king of Persia, "The Eternal, God of heaven...has charged me to build God a house in Jerusalem.... Who is there among you of all of God's people? Let God be with him, and let him go up to Jerusalem...and build the house of the Eternal God of Israel...." (Ezra 1:2–3)

TYPUS ARCHITECTURÆ TEMPLI SPIRITUALIS. *Nehem. 3.* 133.
Nehemias populi invastata Ierusalem relicti afflictionem deploravit et civitate cum Israe, litis contra Insidias Prefectorum vicinorum refecit Nehem C I–3.

The Talmud remembers that this was the beginning of the democratization of the Torah. This moment began Ezra's Reform, a process by which the Torah was copied, placed in every village and hamlet and made part of the daily process of the Jewish people.

What the Talmud Remembers

What the Talmud remembers is that Ezra was the author of ten *Tikkunim*—repairs, fixes, reforms, changes—to the Jewish tradition. These changes are the beginning of the transformation of Judaism from its biblical expression to the Judaism we now live.

Here is a surprise: When you look in the Torah there is just about no Judaism that takes place in either the home or the community. It is a Temple Judaism, a Jerusalem Judaism, a Judaism ruled by a monarch.

If you look just in the Torah you will find no Friday night candles, no Kiddush, no blessing over bread. One does have to put a mezuzah on the door and wear fringes on the corners of a garment, but it is not at all clear that *Shema* is to be said at bedtime, that milk can't be eaten with meat, or that a Passover seder should be held. We learn about the obligation to sacrifice a Paschal lamb (in the Temple). We have matzah and horseradish, but we don't have a *haroset* recipe.

Likewise, local Jewish community is absent. There are no synagogues, no Jewish schools, and no adult education. Everything is pointed toward Jerusalem, toward the Temple. All Jewish events take place there. Then along come Ezra's reforms, and everything changes. The whole balance begins to shift. (Or the description of the balance begins to shift.)

According to the Talmud, Ezra makes these changes:

1. Torah is to be read on Shabbat afternoon (in a synagogue).
2. Torah is to be read on Mondays and Thursdays (in a synagogue).
3. Courts should be held on Mondays and Thursdays (and they should use the Torah to "judge between the people").
4. To get ready for a home Shabbat experience, clothes should be washed on Thursdays.
5. Because it is an aphrodisiac, garlic should be eaten on Fridays (to set up "the double mitzvah").
6. The housewife should rise early to bake bread.
7. A woman must wear a *sinnar* (a garment to protect modesty).
8. A woman must comb her hair before going to the *mikveh*.

7

[Handwritten margin notes:]

EZRA WAS THE AUTHOR OF CHANGES.

THE TORAH DOESN'T DICTATE FRIDAY NIGHT CANDLES NO KIDDUSH, OR BLESSINGS OVER BREAD.

SHEMA IS AT BED TIME.

NOT CLEAR RE: MILK & MEAT,

NO SYNAGOGUES, NO JEWISH SCHOOLS, AND NO ADULT ED.

ALL JEWISH EVENTS TOOK PLACE IN THE TEMPLE.

EZRA CHANGES:

OF COURSE...

OF COURSE

WHY?

"Ezra opened the Torah in the sight of all the people. He was above all the people and when he opened it up, all the people stood." (Nehemiah 8.6)

9. Peddlers (who sell makeup) must be given an exemption to the rule that non-Jews cannot sell to Jews.

10. Men may have moments when they have to go to the *mikveh*, too.

Bava Kama 82a

The first five of these "fixes" reveal our changes; the second five tell different stories.

This displaying of the Torah was the beginning of the custom of *hagbah*. When we hold up the Torah and show it to the congregation, we are recreating an Ezra moment.

The public reading of Torah in every city, neighborhood and village creates the gathering that evolves into regular Jewish worship (if that practice isn't building on worship gatherings that are already in place). We do know from archaeology that there were synagogues before the Babylonian exile, and we suspect that the use of prayers to replace sacrifices was explored during that exile. But those stories are not in the Torah or the rest of the Bible.

What we do know, because the Talmud tells us, is that the public reading of Torah was accompanied by a simultaneous translation of the text, because the Jews who returned no longer spoke Hebrew.

Slowly the *meturgaman*, the translator, was transformed from a person giving his understanding of a passage into a person who read the *targum*, an official translation. The change was motivated by endless arguments over the "meanings" that individuals were sharing. This change, as is often the case, brought about another change. Those who had been honored by the opportunity to transmit the Torah were insulted by their reduction to mere readers. This in turn led to the creation of a new job, *darshan*, "the interpreter." After the reading the *darshan* would deliver a *drash*, a sermon (interpretation). *Midrash*, as a written literature, started out its life as the transcription of these sermons.

Likewise, Talmud grows out of Ezra's "fix" to have courts meet and use the Torah on Mondays and Thursdays.

It happened this way:

Legal cases are rarely neat. Not only do judges have to decide who is telling the truth, they have to bend and stretch the existing laws for the situation they are facing, and they often have to decide between two laws to figure out which one fits.

The Torah tells us:

> A person who fatally strikes another shall be put to death. If that person did not plan the death but it happened by an act of God, there will be cities of refuge where that person can flee to escape the family's desire to take revenge. (Exodus 21.12)

You are a judge.

A fifteen-year-old is skiing recklessly and crashes into another skier. As a result of the injuries received in the accident, the other skier dies.

In American law the fifteen-year-old would be considered a minor, and the charge would be manslaughter, not murder. But a judge using the Torah has got a couple of problems. Nowhere in the Torah is there an overt law that defines the difference between an adult and a minor. (Thirteen as one age of maturity enters the tradition in the Talmud.) Likewise, the Torah gives us murder and accidental death, but there are no shades of murder.

A Jewish judge, working only with the Torah, has to decide if the Torah law should be applied and the "hotdogging" fifteen-year-old should be put to death, or if there are insights that can allow us to create other subcategories (like manslaughter).

Each time such a case was decided, a new "precedent" might be created, and the meaning of the Torah is refined through application. This process of working with the Torah to apply it to actual situations generates a process of "oral" law that grows into the Talmud.

Let Us Honor Ezra

For the rabbis of the Talmud, Ezra was almost as important as Moses. While Moses received both the **Written Torah** and the **Oral Torah**, Ezra restored the **Written Torah** to the Jewish people and began the process through which the **Oral Torah** was organized and passed on.

9

The **Written Torah** includes the Torah, the Prophets and the Writings—the Jewish Bible.

The **Oral Torah** can be thought of in two ways. It can be thought of as the insights and conventions for studying and extracting meaning from the **Written Torah**. Or it can be thought of as the body of knowledge that includes all of the explanations and expansions of the **Written Torah**. The Midrash and the Talmud are the foundational transcriptions of the **Oral Torah**.

- If you believe that God revealed both the Written Torah and the Oral Torah to Moses on the top of Mt. Sinai, then Ezra restored the Torah and reinitiated the process of Oral Torah.

- If you believe that the Oral Law was evolved by Jews studying the Torah, then the process of Oral Law began with Ezra's "fixes."

- If you believe that the Oral Law is actually older than the Written Law, that it starts in the myths and folk traditions that preceded the writing of the Torah, then Ezra began the process of reconnecting the Oral Tradition with the Written—and initiated the process that created the Talmud and finished the Torah.

No matter what you believe, the day Ezra had the Torah read to the entire Jewish people was a critical moment in Jewish history. The Talmud remembers Ezra this way:

Narrator: It has been taught in a baraita (a document from the time of the Mishnah) that Rabbi Yosi said:

Rabbi Yosi: Had Moses not preceded him, Ezra would have been worthy of receiving the Torah for Israel.

Of Moses it is written,

Torah: And Moses went up to God. (Exodus 19.3)

Rabbi Yosi: And of Ezra it is written,

Torah: He, Ezra, went up from Babylon. (Ezra 7.6)

Rabbi Yosi: Just as the "going up" of Moses refers to the "going up to receive the Torah," in the case of Ezra the use of "going up" means that he did the same thing.

Concerning Moses, it is taught:

Torah: And the Eternal commanded me at that time to teach you statutes and judgments; (Deuteronomy 4.14)

Rabbi Yosi: And concerning Ezra, it is stated:

> Torah: For Ezra had prepared his heart to expound the law of the Eternal his God—to do it and to teach Israel statutes and judgments. (Ezra 7.10)

Rabbi Yosi: And even though the Torah was not given through him, like Moses he was involved in "teaching Israel statutes and judgments." The Torah's writing was changed through him...

Sanhedrin 21b

Our Ezra Moment

On the day when Ezra brought the Torah before the Jewish people, we are told that he began by blessing God. The people then responded, "Amen, Amen," and joined in prayer.

(Nehemiah 8.6)

That moment is still very much part of our lives. We relive it at the beginning of every morning and evening service with the words of the *Barekhu*. The leader blesses God and we respond, bowing as we do. Likewise, those same words, that same blessing and response, are used every time we read Torah. They start the blessing before the reading of the Torah.

We have an "Ezra moment" every time we gather as the Jewish community. The *Barekhu* helps us end our individual exiles and become a community. Likewise, every time we take out and read the Torah as a community, we stand with Ezra and know that the Torah has been taken out of the Temple and given to us to study and to apply to our lives.

A Final Note on Ezra: The Ezra of the Talmud is not necessarily a historical figure. He is more a figure of memory. But just as it does not matter if William Shakespeare or Francis Bacon, or Edward de Vere, or Christopher Marlowe, or a committee wrote the works attributed to Shakespeare, what we do know is that these transformations did take place and were associated with him. It is this process of change that concerns us.

The Anatomy of the Talmud Page

Starting to learn Talmud often feels as if we are learning another language. There are lots of names for things that one needs to understand. Here are a few basic terms.

- The Talmud
- Thirty-seven Volumes in Six Orders
- a.k.a. the SHaS (*Shishah Sedarim*)

The SHaS

The encyclopedia-sized set of volumes that take up a whole bookshelf is **THE TALMUD**.

It is also called in *"Gemara Lashon"* (Talmudic slang) **"The GEMARA"** (even though it actually contains both the MISHNAH and the GEMARA.)

It is also known as **"The SHaS."** SHaS is an acronym for *Shishah Sedarim*—"The Six Orders." The thirty-seven volumes of the Babylonian Talmud are divided into six sedarim—"orders" or "divisions."

There is also a Jerusalem or Palestinian Talmud, but it has a different story. We will tell it shortly.

- 1 Volume = A Tractate or a *Masekhet*
- 1 *Daf* = A page (including both sides of the paper)
- 1 Amud = One side of a *Daf*.

The Tractate

When we pull a volume of the TALMUD off the shelf, what we are holding in our hands is a **MASEKHET** or a TRACTATE.

The Daf

When we open up the TRACTATE, we find that we are looking at a **DAF**—a "folio" page. DAF comes from an Akkadian word that means "tablet."

In the Talmud, two sides equal one page. **Page 37** has **side A** and **side B**. This is because the TALMUD's pagination comes from the very early days of printing. Then printers printed one page at a time. First they printed one side of **page 37**, then after it was dry, the other side of **page 37**.

When you write things by hand (like exams in school), most people number each page, not each side. They number the pieces of paper (and then try to do that silly thing with ripping and folding the corner to try to get them to stay together). This is the same practice.   — LOL

It took a few years before they figured out how to print eight pages at a time. When you start dealing with eight-page signatures, then you need individual page numbers to figure out how to fold and cut them.

The Amud

Each side of a **DAF** is called an **AMUD**. AMUD is literally a "pillar" or a "column" and therefore is one "column" of text. **DAF 37** has **AMUD 37a** and **AMUD 37b**.

The first page in every **TRACTATE** is always 2a.

Jacob Neusner explains, "Every Talmudic Tractate begins on page 2; there are no page 1's because there is no beginning. Wherever you start your study, you will feel you have joined a conversation which began long before you came along."

He is telling one truth. Another historical truth is that page 1 was always "the carpet" or "title page." Like your word processor, early scribes (and then early printers) numbered every page.

Talmudic Access Codes

The TALMUD page as we know it was first established by Italian printers between 1520 and 1523 (the Bomberg Edition from Venice).   — "BOMBERG ED" PRINTED BY DANIEL BOMBERG OF ANTWERP (ER) (PUBLISHER)

The standard edition of the TALMUD today, the one that almost all editions of the SHaS use for their Hebrew text, is the Widow and Brothers Romm, Vilna Edition (1880–1886). We use photo images of their typesetting, because their original plates were destroyed in the Holocaust.

The AMUD is the way we access a Talmudic citation. Every edition of the Talmud contains the exact same words on the exact same page. The pagination of the Talmudic text is always identical. Every page in every edition of the Talmud has the same word beginning it.

Mishnah + Gemara

Down the center of every Talmudic page runs the TALMUDIC text. It is a MISHNAH followed by all the GEMARA that discusses it. Then another MISHNAH.

A large מתני MATNAI for MISHNAH and a large גמ GIMMEL MEM for GEMARA divide the flow. A MISHNAH plus all of the GEMARA that discusses it are considered one conversation and called a SUGIA.

The **Mishnah** is the first layer of the Talmud. It was written by rabbis in the Land of Israel between 160 B.C.E. and 210 C.E.

The **Gemara** is the second layer of the Talmud and is a commentary on the Mishnah. It was written in Babylonia between 200 and 500 C.E. There is also a second edition of the Talmud that was started but not finished in the Land of Israel. It is called the Jerusalem Talmud. But when one says "The Talmud," one is talking about the Babylonian Talmud.

Rashi & the Tosafot

Running down the *inside* of every AMUD (closest to the binding) is the commentary of **RASHI**, Rabbi Shlomo Yitzhaki, the dean of Talmudic commentators. He lived in Troyes, France, from 1040 to 1105.

Running down the *outside* of every AMUD are the **TOSAFOT**. The **TOSAFOT** (meaning the "additions") are the additional insights, often from RASHI's students and offspring.

Also clustered around the Talmudic page in small print are a number of other tools and commentaries.

Mishnah + Gemara = Talmud

The Talmud Page Flows in Galleys

On each page of the Talmud the commentaries of RASHI and the TOSAFOT and the thoughts of other commentators run around the outside of the Talmudic text.

RASHI is always on the inside margin. The TOSAFOT always appear in the outside margin.

Every edition of the Talmud has the same words beginning and ending the same page of the text. The words are always "locked" onto a specific page. That is how you find them, not chapter and verse.

Tractate Name

The "tractate" or *masekhet* is named for the overall topic for discussion, though there will be many tangents and related topics. This name reflects the organizing theme of this material.

Chapter Number

The chapter numbers usually come from the Mishnah.

Chapter Name

The name is taken from a key word or two at the beginning of the chapter.

Page Number

This is the *Daf* number only. The *Amud* is obvious from the way the page is facing. The "A" is always the front, the "B" side always the back.

MISHNAH

GEMARA

כיצד הרגל פרק שני בבא קמא כו

Rashi

Rabbi Shlomo Yitzḥaki (Rashi) (1040–1105): Rashi is "the" commentator on the Bible and on the Talmud. He received his early Talmudic training in his native Troyes, France, before traveling to Mainz and Worms (Germany). By the time Rashi returned to Troyes at the age of twenty-five he was considered one of the leading Talmudists of his day. An extremely humble man, Rashi refused to take a rabbinic position. He taught and wrote while earning his livelihood as a wine merchant. Rashi spent most of his life on his Talmud commentary. Rashi gathered around him a number of key students and studied with them daily. His commentaries grew out of their regular study sessions. His commentaries provide the foundation on which most other Jewish commentary is based. He marked the trail others follow through this material. His later years were marred by the excruciating suffering of the Jews during the first crusade in 1096, when many important Jewish communities were destroyed.

Collected into the Tosafot were:

Rabbi Yakov ben Meir ("Rabbenu Tam") (c. 1100–1171): He is Rashi's grandson and lived in the French town of Ramerupt. **Rabbi Samuel ben Meir (The RaShBaM)** (c. 1080–c. 1158): He is another grandson of Rashi's and the brother of Rabbenu Tam. He was also the author of a famous Torah commentary. **Rabbi Isaac of Dampierre (The RI):** A nephew of Rabbenu Tam and the Rashbam who lived in France during the 12th century. **Rabbi Samson ben Abraham of Sens:** Rabbi Samson was another 12th-century Frenchman who eventually moved to Jerusalem. He was a student of Rabbi Isaac of Dampierre. **Rabbi Meir ben Barukh of Rothenburg:** Rabbi Meir was born in Worms, Germany, around 1225 and died in 1293 while being held for ransom by the Emperor Rudolph. He made significant contributions to Jewish civil law.

Mesoret Ha-ShaS

This tool was assembled by Rabbi Joshua Boaz Barukh (1518–1555), a Spanish exile living in Italy. It is a cross-reference to other places in the Talmud where the same quote appears.

Ein Mishpat/Ner Mitzvah (The Wellspring of Justice/The Lamp of Commandment)

This is another set of marginal notes by Rabbi Joshua Boaz Barukh, this time connecting the Talmud's text to various legal codes like the *Mishneh Torah* and the *Shulḥan Arukh*.

Torah Or (The Law Is a Light)

This is the third set of notes by Rabbi Joshua Boaz Barukh. This one gives the sources of all the biblical quotations.

Other commentators included in the Vilna Edition of the Talmud were:

Rabbenu Hananel (990–1050) (Kairowan, Tunisia): This commentary comes from the source closest to the actual Babylonian *Ge'onim*. They were the direct heirs of the Babylonian academies. *Sefer ha-Mafte-aḥ* (**The Book with "The Key"**) (Rabbi Nissim ben Jacob) (died c. 1062) (Kairowan, Tunisia): This commentary identifies obscure allusions to other places in Talmudic literature. *Tosafot Yeshanim:* This commentary presents various alternative versions of the *Tosafot* from different sources. **Rabbenu Gershom Mainz Commentary** (died 1028) (Mainz, Germany): This commentary was compiled by the students of Rabbi Gershom ben Judah, "the Light of the Exile." **Tosafot RID** (Rabbi Isaiah ben Mali diTrani, the Elder) (13th century) (Trani, Italy): This commentary summarizes the laws that appear in the Talmud. *Shittah Mekubbetzet* (Rabbi Bezalel ben Abraham Ashkenazi) (16th century) (Egypt and Jerusalem): This is a collection of variant readings of the texts of the Talmud, Rashi and the Tosafot.

Found in the Glosses to the Vilna Edition:

These were comments that were copied from the handwritten notes that the authors inscribed in the margins of their personal copies of the Talmud. **Rabbi Elijah ben Solomon, the Vilna Ga'on** (1720–1797) (Vilna, Lithuania). *Hagahot Ha-Baḥ* (Rabbi Joel Sirkes) (1561–1640) (Poland). **Rabbi Isaiah (Pick) Berlin** (1725–1799) (Breslau, Germany). *Gilyon Ha-Shas* (meaning "In the Margins of the Talmud") (Rabbi Akiva Eger) (1761–1837) (Posen, Prussia).

From Ezra to the Mishnah

This story is found in the Talmud:

Narrator:	Our Rabbis taught in a BARAITA (a rabbinic tradition from the time of the Mishnah):
BARAITA:	A certain heathen once came before Shammai and asked:
Heathen:	How many Torahs do you have?
Narrator:	He said:
Shammai:	Two: the Written Torah and the Oral Torah.
Narrator:	He said:
Heathen:	I will believe you with respect to the Written, but not with respect to the Oral Torah; convert me only on the basis of the Written Torah.
Narrator:	But Shammai scolded him and drove him away in anger. When the heathen went before Hillel with those same conditions, Hillel accepted him as a conversion student. On the first day, he taught him:
Hillel:	Alef, Bet, Gimmel, Dalet.
Narrator:	The following day he reversed the order. The heathen said:
Heathen:	But yesterday you taught them to me the other way!
Narrator:	Hillel said:
Hillel:	You have to trust me when it comes to the truth about Alef–Bet. You should also trust me about the truth of the Oral Torah, too. Shabbat 31a

Understanding **Oral Torah** is the key to understanding **Talmud**.

We know that in one way or another, Ezra was responsible for the reintroduction of the **Written Torah**. We learned that he was responsible for the survival and growth of the **Oral Torah**, too. The Talmud tells the story of the preservation and development of the **Oral Torah** this way:

The Talmudic Telling

Mishnah: **Moses received Torah at Sinai and passed it on to Joshua. Joshua handed it down to the elders, the elders handed it to the prophets, and the prophets handed it to the men of the Great Assembly.** Pirkei Avot 1:1

This text traces the progression of the Oral Torah from Moses to the rabbis.

In the *Mishneh Torah* Moses Maimonides fills in a little more detail on the chain of the tradition that led from Mt. Sinai to the Talmud.

Maimonides: Moses personally wrote down the whole Torah
before he died. He gave one to each tribe and
placed one in the ark. But he did not write
down the interpretations of the Torah. Instead
he taught this orally to the elders, to Joshua,
and to all of Israel...

Joshua taught Oral Torah his whole life.
Many elders learned it from him.
Eli learned it from those elders...
Samuel learned it from Eli and his court.
David learned it from Samuel and his court...

Elijah learned the Oral Torah from Ahiah of Shiloh.
Ahiah had come out of Egypt as a child and
learned from Moses and the Elders.
Elisha learned Oral Torah from Elijah and his court.

Yehoyada learned from Elisha and his court.
Zachariah learned from Elisha and his court.
Hosea learned from Zachariah and his court.
Amos learned from Hosea and his court.
Isaiah learned from Amos and his court.
Micah learned from Isaiah and his court.
Joel learned from Isaiah and his court...
(and so on) until Barukh learned from Jeremiah
and his court.
Barukh taught the Oral Law to Ezra.

Ezra's court were called "The men of the Great Assembly."
Simon the Just was part of Ezra's court.
His is one of the oldest names mentioned in the Talmud.

That is one of the ways of telling the story. Here is another.

A Historical Telling

In the mid-300s B.C.E. Alexander the Great conquered most of the known world, including Judea (332 B.C.E.) (soon to be Palestina). This brought about great economic changes, including the growth of the city and the rise of a middle (merchant) class. Oodles of farm kids left home and moved to the city. Over this period the local economy moved from an agrarian base to being an industrial and mercantile center.

City Life

The Land of Israel had always been a trading center, doing business with those merchants going back and forth between the Nile Delta and the Fertile Crescent. Since the time of King David, particularly linked with the Phoenicians, Jewish merchants had been trading all over the known world. But with the super-charging brought about by the international Hellenist economy, life in the Land of Israel took on an industrial cast. Israel became a center for weaving and especially dyeing. We owned the secret to a particular shade of purple (the one used on the fringes of the tallit) that royalty and the rich were seeking. Some scholars suggest that we invented glass blowing. But adding to the economy now was industrial farming, the creation of wine, date honey, and olive oil, all of which became major exports.

Before Alexander Israel was, for the most part, a sheep farming community. In this new world of city-states, the farm kids discovered a whole new way of life—city life. There were now lots of people living close together in a new kind of community. There was for the first time light after dark because people earned a living by selling oil and wood. But most exciting of all—there was now **leisure time**.

Leisure Time

The Greeks were the masters of leisure time, and these farm kids, who used to work from dawn to dusk and who couldn't afford light after dark, were suddenly taken by the new possibilities. There were the baths, the theater and athletics. There were schools, dances, music, orgies, banquets and lots of other pastimes.

Some Jews followed the Greeks' lead. They were called the **Hellenizers** and they believed that leisure time should be used for pleasure. Other Jews, the **Hasidim**, the Pious Ones, felt that free time should be used to study the Torah, to come closer to God and to make the world a place for all to come to live in peace and prosperity. They centered much of their lives around the newly evolving synagogues.

To a large degree, priestly kids and other longtime city-dwelling families, the old wealth, became **Hellenizers**, while the ranks of the **Hasidim** were made up of new-to-city farm kids who replanted their village faith and traditions in the big city.

Hanukkah

The **Hanukkah war**, in **164 B.C.E.**, was in reality a civil war between **Hasidim** and **Hellenizers** that was exacerbated by a slightly mad Syrian despot, Antiochus III. It grew into a revolution. In its wake temporary religious freedom was won. However, the real victory was that of the **Hasidim**, who gained control over the Temple and its practices, as well as the Sanhedrin, the national religious decision-making body. We can't say for sure that Ezra's students became the **Hasidim**, but they clearly were his extension.

By **63 B.C.E.** the positions remained constant, but the names had changed. The foreign rulers were now the Romans. Similar to the Hellenizers was a political party called the **Sadducees**, many of whom came from rich priestly families. The middle-class religious renewal group was called the **Pharisees**. Starting around **30 B.C.E.** the Pharisees began collecting their teachings and those of their ancestors and formalizing their position. This process of collection was completed around **210 C.E.** and became the **Mishnah**. Rabbinic Judaism is Pharisaic Judaism.

In 70 C.E. the Temple was destroyed, **Jerusalem was destroyed** and the center of Jewish life shifted elsewhere. It first went to **Yavneh**, a small city with a rabbinic academy, located essentially where Ben Gurion Airport stands today. Here, under **Rabban Yohanan ben Zakkai**, the Jews began a process of reconstructing Judaism without a Temple or a king. Rabbinic Judaism was now fully in power.

In 132 c.e., under the leadership of **Bar Kokhba** and backed by the religious authority of **Rabbi Akiva** and others, the Jews successfully rebelled against Rome and won a short period of freedom. By 135 the revolt had ended, new persecutions had begun and Jewish life in Judea was all but over. This created big pressure to complete the task of collecting and organizing the existing law codes. Too few students were left to sustain the process.

By 210 Judah the Prince, the head of the Sanhedrin, completed the redaction of the **Mishnah**. Rabbi Judah lived in a time of relative peace. But with the memory of the Hadrianic persecutions that had followed the Roman victory over Bar Kokhba (the holocaust of his era), he committed himself to writing down the Oral Law as a kind of time capsule protection of the knowledge. Judah and his Sanhedrin worked in the Galilee.

Essentially, as soon as the Mishnah collection was finished, they "photocopied" the text and "express mailed" it to Babylonia. There it was received by all of the rich Jewish families who had never returned to the Land of Israel. Quickly the center of Jewish life shifted there. Talmudic academies flourished in Babylonia for 300 years, culminating in the completion of the *Gemara*.

The Written Torah/The Oral Torah

Written Torah: The *Torah she-b'Khtav*

Most of the time the Talmud calls it "MIKRA," meaning "the reading" or "the text." The Rabbis also call it *Torah she-b'Khtav*, the WRITTEN TORAH, and by that they mean the whole Bible. The last book in the Bible (historically) is Chronicles II. It ends with the story of the Babylonian Exile, 586 B.C.E., and the return. The Talmud credits Ezra (circa 450 B.C.E.) with writing this book. Sometime just after 430 B.C.E. the Bible was completed.

The Bible Is Divided into Three Sections

The Hebrew name for the Bible is the תנ״ך *Ta'NaKh*. This is an acronym made up of the first letters of three Hebrew words: תּוֹרָה *Torah* (the Law), נְבִיאִים *Nevi'im* (the Prophets), כְּתוּבִים *K'tuvim* (Writings). The Hebrew Bible is a library of twenty-four books that are divided into these three sections.

תּוֹרָה *Torah*	נְבִיאִים *Nevi'im*	כְּתוּבִים *K'tuvim*
	The Prophets	**The Writings**
Genesis		Psalms
Exodus	Joshua	Proverbs
Leviticus	Judges	Job
Numbers	Samuel	Song of Songs
Deuteronomy	Kings	Ruth
	Isaiah	Lamentations
	Jeremiah	Ecclesiastes
	Ezekiel	Esther
	The Twelve	Daniel
	Prophets	Ezra/Nehemiah
		Chronicles

Tanakh Chart There are twenty-four books in this chart. The Christian Bible (and most Jewish editions of the Hebrew Bible) winds up with thirty-nine books by breaking out each of the twelve "minor" prophets into his own book and by dividing Samuel, Kings, Chronicles and Ezra/Nehemiah into two books each. The order of books in the Christian Bible is also different.

The *Torah she-b'Al Peh*: Layer One

Here is a second look at the history of the Mishnah. This one is sociological.

The Mishnah/The Tanna'im

As soon as the **Written Torah** was completed, the process of interpretation and application went into high gear. We now move into what is called the **Oral Torah**. In classes and courtrooms, in sanctuaries and academies, whenever Torah was read or studied or argued or applied, the wisdom revealed to Moses continued to grow and be clarified. Between about 160 B.C.E. and 210 C.E. in **Eretz Yisrael**, a group of rabbinic scholars we call the **Tanna'im** developed a detailed and well-passed-on **Oral Tradition**, much of which came to be written down in the MISHNAH.

The **Tanna'im** all had day jobs. They were sandal-makers and tailors, merchants and even rubbish collectors. They gathered in the **Bet Midrash** (the House of Study) after work to study and argue. Often they brought the individual traditions from their towns of origin and compared them.

Facing Modernity

Much of the work of the **Tanna'im** involved confronting modernity. Greco-Roman culture forced the Torah to adapt to a brand-new world. Fitting into city life, adapting to an international marketplace, facing Greco-Roman thought, challenged many of the Torah's laws that were designed to fit a rural, agrarian culture. Here are a few examples:

- The Torah speaks (for the most part) of a barter economy where business involves trading one thing for another. Greco-Roman culture used money. International trade often used the "idea" of money where loans and profits took place "on the books" and not with the passing of actual coins. Where "no interest" is a good rule for farmers, "no interest" is a much harder rule for a trader who needs to buy on margin and then sell for a profit.

- The Torah speaks of neighbors as people whose farm is near yours. Suddenly, when you lived in a city, when your neighbors lived above you and below you, or on the other side of the same apartment courtyard, the meaning of "good neighbor" changed. How late at night you can play your music is an ethical issue whose solution is not easy to find directly in the Torah.

- When the Torah gave rules for divorce that demanded personal contact, but the husband might now be a merchant who traveled the whole known world to sell his wares, some accommodations or adaptations were needed.

The list goes on and on. To a large degree, Talmud (and Mishnah in particular) is the record of how you take the laws and teachings of the Torah and bring them forward into the modern world, even though it was a modern world circa 100 B.C.E.

Living in Cities

Two of these needed adaptations seemed to speed the process along. Both of them had to do with food. The first was a "*kashrut*" issue, but it was not about meat. The Torah makes it a big deal that to be "fit for Jewish use," grain had to be tithed. The right portions had to be taken out for the Temple and for the poor. When you no longer grow your own food but buy it in the marketplace, you have to trust that the farmer did this. If you want to be absolutely sure, you have to take the matter into your own hands. Soon,

tithing cooperatives were in operation. These groups either supervised their own harvests or retithed the grain they bought, just to make sure. The second issue had to do with ovens. When you lived in a Greco-Roman apartment, the ovens were on the outside. In order to carry food from the oven on Shabbat (and not have it count as work) you needed to make the outside part of your house. You did that with a fence (an *eruv*) that closed off the space, and with a communal meal once in a while that made everyone who lived in the courtyard into one unit. These groups were called <u>H</u>avurot (that's where the name comes from), and they were part of the bonding process that gathered and unified the **Tanna'im**, those who created the **Mishnah**.

A Written Oral Tradition

For a long time it was a rule that the **Oral Torah** could not be written down. The rabbis thought that it was like a mobile. When you write something down, it has an order. Some things go first and other things come later. The rabbis believed that the Torah was meant to be associative, with everything having the possibility to connect TO everything else. To write it down would be like welding a mobile in one position.

Think of it this way.

- **Linear Memory:** When I was a child (and some of you are probably my age), we were taught to use 3x5 cards in the library to take notes. You would then go home, stack the notes, usually three facts to a paragraph, and then make an outline. The report needed a beginning, a middle and an end. Order was important. To this day I often know that something I was looking for in a book was at the bottom of a right-hand page near a chocolate smudge.

- **Associative Memory:** There is a youth group game called a sing down. The idea is simple. The leader asks, "How many songs can you think of with the word blue in the title?" Suddenly, you go into random search mode (like the player on an old jukebox going back and forth picking out records). You run a list of show tunes and then jump to the Beatles. You do "Jump Blues" and then head to nursery rhymes. Slowly you scan through all of the songs you know, looking for as many matches as possible.

The rabbis believed that every Torah verse could connect in some way to every other verse. They were always looking for associations. They used Oral Torah to keep things in the realm of memory and out of outlines. They wanted Torah study to always be a sing down.

Only when things got desperate did they agree to write things down. After Bar Kokhba came the Hadrianic persecutions to get even with the Jews for both revolting and winning.

The Roman historian Dio Cassius tells us:

> Very few of them in fact survived. Fifty of their most important outposts and 985 of their most famous villages were razed to the ground, and 580,000 men were slain in various raids and battles, and the number of those who perished by famine, disease and fire was past finding out.
>
> Thus nearly the whole of Judea was made desolate...

Hadrian completely leveled Jerusalem and built a pagan city in its place. He renamed the land Philistina (after the Philistines) and sowed salt in the soil, destroying the ecology of the land and turning "milk and honey" into the desert we now know. He executed Rabbi Akiva and the other martyrs we read about on Yom Kippur afternoon and killed lots of Jews.

Having reached an emergency situation, and being afraid that all of this learning would be lost, the **Tanna'im** began to write down all they knew—sort of as a time capsule—so that it would not vanish. In a three-generation effort, a teacher-to-student-to-student handoff, the **Mishnah** was drawn together and edited. Before he was executed, Rabbi Akiva established the six orders, Rabbi Meir began to structure the material within them, and Rabbi Yehudah ha-Nasi created the final document.

MISHNAH = "The Teaching" or "The Re-teaching." It comes from a Hebrew root that is also used for both the number two and "instruction." The lesson is simple: either teaching or learning requires repetition. **Tanna'im** comes from that same linguistic origin.

Tanna'im = "The Repeaters." It also has its origins in an Aramaic term that means "to hand down orally," "to study," or "to teach." The **Tanna'im** are the "two-timers," the rabbis who, by re-teaching the Torah, grew, expanded and adapted it.

The Mishnah

The Mishnah is a fairly straightforward law code. It is divided into six *Sedarim* (orders). Inside these are tractates or *masekhta'ot*. When you buy a Mishnah, usually each *Seder* is a book, and the tractates are like chapters.

Zera'im (Seeds)—Agricultural Law

Mo'ed (Festivals)—Holiday Law

Nashim (Women)—Family Law

Nezikin (Damages)—Torts

Kodashim (Sacred Things)—Temple Law

Tohorot (Purifications)—Laws of Purity

From the Mishnah to the Gemara

The Torah she-b'Al Peh: Part Two

The Gemara/The Amora'im

After 200 C.E. the center of Jewish life moved to Babylonia, to the Talmudic academies there, places like Sura, Pumbedita, Ma<u>h</u>oza and Nehardeah. There Jewish life and scholarship flourished for 300 years.

The Babylonian community was a rich community, and they were able to create full-time schools, Ivy League *Yeshivot* (academies) where full-time students studied with a full-time faculty. This was completely different than the world of the Mishnah, which was an after-work or between-harvest, part-time reality. The rabbis of the Mishnah had been the **Tanna'im**, the "repeaters"; these full-time Babylonian Talmudists were now called **Amora'im**, the speakers.

The switch from part-time to full-time made a big difference. So did the distance in time and geography that **Amora'im** felt from the rabbis who wrote the Mishnah. The **Gemara** emerges as a very different work. Intellectually, it spends most of its time trying to understand the Mishnah. The **Amora'im** are constantly

Tractates of the Talmud

Zera'im (Seeds)	Mo'ed (Festivals)	Nashim (Women)
Berakhot	Shabbat	Yevamot
Pe'ah*	Eruvin	Ketubbot
Demai*	Pesa<u>h</u>im	Nedarim
Kilayim*	Shekalim*	Nazir
Shevi'it*	Yoma	Sotah
Terumot*	Sukkah	Gittin
Ma'aserot*	Betzah	Kiddushin
Ma'aser Sheni*	Rosh ha-Shanah	
<u>H</u>allah*	Ta'anit	
Orlah*	Megillah	
Bikkurim*	Mo'ed Katan	
	<u>H</u>agigah	

asking "How did they come up with that ruling?" or "Where did that idea come from?" The rabbis of the Gemara sense a gap between their understandings and the core knowledge that the **Tanna'im** had. The **Amora'im** are constantly trying to reconstruct the reasoning and context that had been clear to the rabbis of the Mishnah.

The Mishnah is a terse work. For the most part, the **Tanna'im** state laws and do little else. The **Gemara** benefits from time. It evolves as a celebration in tangents and associations. It reads like a great conversation that wanders away and then comes back to topic after topic. While the Mishnah is a log of key rules, the **Gemara** is a wonderful dinner party where great minds explore great ideas.

By 350 C.E. life in Babylonia began to disintegrate. There was a swirl of chaos whirling between the Byzantines and the Magi, pro-Zoroastrian pagans; it was a chaos that by 700 C.E. would give birth to Islam.

Nezikin (Damages)	Kodashim (Sacred Things)	Tohorot (Purifications)
Bava Kamma	Zevahim	Kelim
Bava Metzia	Menahot	Oholot
Bava Batra	Hullin	Nega'im
Sanhedrin	Bekhorot	Parah
Makkot	Arakhin	Tohorot
Shevu'ot	Temurah	Mikva'ot
Eduyyot*	Keritot	Niddah
Avodah Zarah	Me'ilah	Makhshirin
Avot*	Tamid	Zavim
Horayot	Middot	Tevul Yom
	Kinnim	Yadayim
		Uktzin

Those with an * have a Mishnah but no Gemara.

313 C.E.   The Roman Emperor Constantine recognizes the Christian religion and moves his capital from Rome to Constantinople in 324.

351 C.E.   Gallus, the Eastern Roman Emperor, begins what is basically a religious crusade against the Jews in the Land of Israel. Many of the *Amora'im* in *Eretz Yisrael* flee to Babylon.

392 C.E.   Ravina and Rav Ashi begin the process of editing the Babylonian Talmud.

395 C.E.   Enter the Visigoths (a.k.a. barbarians), and Jews flee from Greece. The Roman Empire is dying fast, and the Dark Ages are coming.

414 C.E.   Jews are expelled from Alexandria.

427 C.E.   Rav Ashi dies, and the Gemara is just about edited.

429 C.E.   The Roman Emperor Theodosious II shuts down the Jewish government in Babylonia by forbidding the raising of funds for the Nasi, the leader.

455 C.E.   The Jews of Babylonia are forbidden from keeping Shabbat by King Yesdegerd (who is later killed by a snake).

The Vandals (more barbarians) sack and loot Rome.

469 C.E.   Firuz the Wicked, son of King Yesdegerd, arrests and executes three leading Jewish figures.

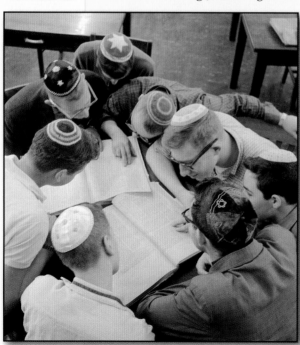

474 C.E.   All synagogues in Babylon are closed, and many Jewish children are handed over to pagan priests.

475 C.E.   The Talmud is completed. The final editing is done.

486 C.E.   More persecutions are prepetrated when Firuz dies. His successor imposes a religious cult on all Babylonia.

GEMARA = From an Aramaic root that means the "to study."

AMORA'IM = From a root that means "speak," the **Amora'im** are the speakers, the lecturers, and the interpreters.

The Talmud

The Torah of Jaywalking

A Parable on the Difference between Mishnah & Gemara

In a town we'll call Smallville, on a street we will call Elm Street, a child is killed by a Stealth Ice Cream truck (one that wasn't playing music to attract customers) when he runs off the lawn and between two parked cars into the "end zone" to catch a long bomb thrown by his older brother. Smallville is shocked. The town council calls a special meeting. The town passes a law setting a $500 fee for crossing a street in the wrong way (jaywalking). The law carefully talks about intersections, crosswalks and lights. It tells the police and the judges just who should receive a ticket.

Smallville Ordinance 3222156: It is lawful for a pedestrian to cross a street only at an intersection or at any other place where either crossing lights or painted crosswalks indicate that crossing is permitted. Any other form of crossing a street shall be deemed as jaywalking and shall be punishable by a $500.00 fine.

The law does not contain a rationale. It does not explain that the jaywalking laws were designed to save lives. All of those issues, the reasoning and the debate, took place in the town council (and might be part of its records) but didn't need to be part of the actual ordinance.

Twenty years later Mrs. Kent is cited for jaywalking. She had crossed Elm Street from her house to the house across the street at 2:00 in the morning in order to borrow some sugar from Aunt Bee to finish the surprise cake she was baking for her son Clark's birthday. Clark was about to leave town and become a reporter for a major metropolitan newspaper. She refuses to pay the fine, arguing, "The intent of the law was public safety, and at 2 A.M. there is no question of public safety." In the courtroom there is a need to reconstruct the "intent" of the law and decide if the 2 A.M. case should change the enforcement of the jaywalking statute.

The judge sends to town hall for the minutes of the town council meeting at which the original ordinance was passed.

Mayor: It isn't the money. It is the safety. We don't care about the income, but we do care that parents teach their kids to be careful.

Gomer: They why not just have Officer Friendly go to the public schools and teach the children about pedestrian safety?

Sheriff Andy Taylor: That would help some, but what we need to do is to get parents involved. This fine would really motivate parental involvement, because they would have to pay if their kids crossed unsafely.

Floyd: I don't always walk to the corner, but I do cross safely. Are you going to make me walk to the crosswalk every time I go to get a soda?

Sheriff Taylor: Yes, Floyd, we are. It is a price you'll have to pay in order to keep our kids safe. That is unless you want to buy a five-hundred-dollar-and-thirty-five cent soda.

Mayor: Now our judges will be reasonable about this fine, applying it with discretion. After all, our intent is to ensure public safety, not create financial hardship.

The judge, having read the town council records, writes the following opinion as part of his verdict.

The following facts are clear. First, Mrs. Kent readily admits crossing a street, not at a crosswalk, and therefore is technically guilty of jaywalking. She has stipulated to these facts, and so our only question is this: Should this court intervene in the fine she has to pay?

The statute is clear. It states, "Any other form of crossing a street shall be deemed as jaywalking and shall be punishable by a $500.00 fine." It has a "one crime—one penalty" view of jaywalking that would seem to leave little room for this court to change the law no matter how much that is what we want to do. We would be stuck,

---

unable to do anything but enforce the law as written—except that the minutes of the town council meeting actually allow us to go back and reconstruct the intent of the framers of this law.

The town council begins with a discussion of various models that might make the streets of Smallville safe for our children. Some of these suggestions are interesting.

Barney Fife suggested that we ban cars from all of the Smallville streets and turn the town into "one of these new-fangled pedestrian malls."

Opie: If the problem was an ice cream truck running without music on, why don't we make it a law that ice cream trucks always have to have their music or bell playing when they are moving?

Thelma Lou suggested building fences along the sidewalks to make it impossible to cross at any point other than intersections. When asked about driveways, she said, "I think I will have to think it over."

It is clear from this conversation that the intent of this law was indeed safety, but that still doesn't make it clear that I have the power to alter the fine that the law imposes.

Then we come to the statement by the mayor, who said, "Now our judges will be reasonable about this fine, applying it with discretion. After all, our intent is to ensure public safety, not create financial hardship." This statement, part of the official record, makes it clear that the law was created with the belief that judges would interpret the application of fines and have the power to adjust them based on the situation and the need.

Therefore, in this case, I find Mrs. Kent guilty and sentence her to bake one of her famous pies to be part of lunch on our annual jury appreciation day.

MISHNAH is a lot like the town ordinance—it gives the rule without much explanation as to the intent or the context.

GEMARA is a lot like the judge's opinion, which goes to great effort to reconstruct the underlying reasoning and context for the law. The Gemara—like the judge's opinion—is designed to clarify the law's application.

There is a third kind of material in the Talmud. It is called a **Baraita**. (This is pronounced "*ba-right-ta*" and does not sound like a Mexican food.)

A **baraita** is like the town council minutes that were (a) written by the same folks who wrote the rules, but (b) not made part of the rule book.

A **baraita** is a piece of "Torah" (insight) that was created by the **Tanna'im** (the rabbis of the Mishnah) but not included in it. These fragments of teaching were kept alive in the Oral Torah, used by the **Amora'im** as part of their arguments and as part of the data they used for unpacking the Mishnah. Often the Gemara seems like a stitching together of **beraitot** (more than one **baraita**).

How to Use a Baraita

The **Amora'im** thought that **Beraitot** were almost just as important as **Mishna'ot.** They gave them almost equal weight, even though we might think that the ones chosen to be in the **Mishnah** would be much more important (and these are just runner-up teachings).

This explanation seems to help:

A disc jockey is given the chance to pick sixty classic hits from the 1960s to fill up a BOXED SET of '60s music. She spends a lot of time picking and choosing a good collection out of some three thousand "top 100" records from that ten-year period. She picks her version of the best. She leaves out some songs she loves because, for instance, it is unfair to have more than two songs by the Supremes. *Alice's Restaurant*, a pivotal tune, is left out because it is eighteen minutes long. Everything included is a greatest hit, but if not included a song isn't necessarily an "unclassic" or a "non-greatest hit." Lots of people will still hum it and know it—and it will still show up in her radio playlist.

That is exactly how the **Amora'im** treat **Beraitot.**

Talmudic Tool Box

The following four "insights" will be really helpful once you start to study Talmud. Two of them have to do with the way that the Talmud views the biblical text; two of them have to do with the way that Talmudic arguments proceed.

1. The Torah Is Like a Zipped File

If you want to understand the Torah the way the rabbis did, you need to start with one basic idea: God taught Moses two kinds of Torah, the Written Torah and the Oral Torah.

- **The Written Torah** is not only the Torah (the Five Books of Moses) but also includes the rest of the Bible, the Prophets and the Writings.

- **The Oral Torah** includes the Talmud, the Midrash and later codes and commentaries, right up to the latest pieces of Jewish wisdom that are now being written. But here is the catch. Do not think of Oral Torah as commentary on the Torah. Do not think of it as additions and transformations. None of that is the way the rabbis understood Oral Torah. Rather, think of it as a slow unfolding of the wisdom embedded in the Torah.

Think of a zipped or a compressed computer file. That metaphor will help. God has Moses up on Mt. Sinai for forty days and forty nights. In that time God has to teach Moses enough Torah to last until the messiah comes—until the messianic era is actual. It takes nine months to write down a Torah scroll. Moses has to (according to the Midrash) write down the entire Torah plus master a complex secondary literature in a little under six weeks. God's secret weapon is the nature of the Oral Torah. It is like a time-release capsule, set to release as needed.

A Zipped File Works Like This

Here is the way it works. If I want to shorten the word "running" to the least number of keystrokes, I can compress or "zip" it. I can use "search and replace." I tell the computer to substitute a capital G for every use of "ing." The word "running" is now "runnG." A capital letter at the end of a word is never a usual usage. Likewise, I can tell the computer to make every double letter a single capital. "running" is now "ruNG." If I give the computer an English dictionary, I can remove the vowel "u" because "ranning," "renning," "rinning," and "ronning" are not words. An underlined "r" will indicate a missing vowel. Therefore I can compress "running" into "rNG." To turn "rNG" back into running I just run my search and replace program in reverse. To make sense of the "short version," I need to know the rules for decompressing. You know the experience of sitting and watching your computer do just that with much bigger and more complicated rules. This happens every time the blue line creeps across your screen showing you the percentage of the process that has been completed.

The rabbis believed that the Written Torah was the zipped/compressed version of the Oral Torah. All of the Jewish law that the Jewish people would need, all of the interpretations of the text, all of the meanings that would come into play were there, ready to be unfolded from the text. What Moses learned on Mt. Sinai was two things: the text of the Written Torah and the rules for expanding it into the Oral Torah. One of the assumptions in this process is that we often find answers in the Torah, and are able to make sense of them, just when we need them. Often our perception of the problem allows an answer we already had but didn't quite perceive to come into focus. That is the way God revealed enough Torah to last us until the final redemption.

How You Read

You need not accept this vision of the Torah. Many important theologians and teachers reject it. But you will need to be able to look through its lens, because all of rabbinic Judaism starts with it as a given. That is the way the Talmud understands its work, and that is the way the Talmud reads Torah.

2. The Two Sisters

Here is a great way of understanding how this "unpacking" of Torah works. This joke helps to make it clear. It was sent to me by a "Joke-of-the-Day" website that one of my students signed me up for (against my will).

The Joke

Two sisters are just about ready to lose their farm. One of the sisters takes their last $400 and goes off to buy a bull. The second sister will come with the truck and the trailer and pick up the bull when she gets a telegram from her sister. They believe that as a stud the bull can save the enterprise. She finds the perfect bull and buys it for $398. She then goes to the telegraph office, tells the story to the operator, and discovers that telegrams cost a dollar a word. The operator asks, "What are you going to do? You only have two dollars." The sister says, "No problem. Send my sister the word "Comfortable." The operator says, "I don't get it." The sister says, "It's simple. My sister reads very, very slowly."

The Idea

The Torah has no vowels and no punctuation—that makes it really easy to "revowel" words and turn one of them into another. Likewise, it is easy to divide words and join words in very different ways. The rabbis evolved lots of ways of turning "**comfortable**" into "**come-for-da-bull**." They did so based on two assumptions:

a. The Torah was designed to be a "zipped file." Alternate readings and multiple understandings are some of the ways that God embedded the Oral Torah in the Written Torah.

b. Nothing in the Torah is a mistake. Everything that looks problematic is really a clue to "dig here." When something looks wrong, when something looks extraneous or contradictory, this is really a signal to use the "decoder ring" and figure out the larger message that God embedded in just a few words.

An Example

Here is the very last part of the tractate of *Berakhot* (Blessings). It is a very famous "come for the bull" understanding.

Narrator: Rabbi Eleazar said in the name of Rabbi Ḥanina:

Rabbi Eleazar: Students of the sages increase peace in the world, as it says,

Torah: All your children shall be taught of the Eternal,
and great shall be the peace of your children. Isaiah 54.13

Rabbi Eleazar: Don't read the word as בָּנָיִךְ banayik (your children) but rather
understand it as בּוֹנָיִךְ bonayik (your builders). Berakhot 64a

The message here is clear: Your children can be your builders if you teach them Torah.

3. The Tarzan Movie

My friend and teacher, Yosi Gordon, has always explained one of the difficulties in understanding Talmud with this metaphor.

Imagine one of those Tarzan-comes-to-New York movies. He is in a Manhattan penthouse and hears this simple conversation:

a: That's the phone.

b: I am in the shower.

a: Okay.

Tarzan, with his new understanding of Manhattan culture, translates the conversation this way:

a: That is an instrument for speaking across long distances over a wire.

b: I am in a glass box having water dumped over my head.

a: That is a satisfactory condition.

The couple involved in the conversation, however, understand it this way:

a: The phone is ringing. I'm cooking. Can you get it?

b: Sorry, but I am in the shower and I'd get water all over the carpet.

a: Never mind. I'll turn down the stove and answer it.

The Talmud is written, for the most part, in conversational shorthand. We are often like Tarzan, stuck figuring out the meaning of a conversation whose words we have, but whose contexts and idioms are remote. We are regularly left filling in words and concepts to make sense out of the words recorded in the text.

When you read most Talmudic translations, they are filled with lots of words (written in brackets) or with a combination of **bold words** and *italics* to indicate all the words that the translator is filling in. In our translations we are idiomatic, giving you what you need to understand (and not worrying about the technical precision of academic translation).

Rehydrating the Mishnah

When you study Mishnah, it is just as if you were borrowing someone else's lecture notes. They are written in a kind of shorthand that is clear to the author, but you are often stuck trying to reconstruct the lesson from the minimal language that is on the page.

Not only is this our problem, but often it is also the problem of the **Amora'im**, the rabbis who wrote the Gemara. Frequently we see their best guesses at the meaning of a Mishnah.

Here is an example of the way this works.

> **MISHNAH: THE PRIMARY LABORS ARE FORTY LESS ONE: SOWING, PLOUGHING, REAPING, BINDING SHEAVES, THRESHING, WINNOWING, SELECTING, GRINDING, SIFTING, KNEADING, BAKING...** Shabbat 7.2

If we "rehydrated" this Mishnah and applied the "Tarzan" principle, it would come out like this:

> **Mishnah: What kinds of things are considered to be "work" and are therefore forbidden on Shabbat?**
>
> **There are thirty-nine categories of things that are considered work.**
>
> **Eleven of them have to do with producing bread. These are: (1) sowing, (2) ploughing, (3) reaping, (4) binding sheaves, (5) threshing, (6) winnowing, (7) selecting, (8) grinding, (9) sifting, (10) kneading, (11) baking...** Shabbat 7.2

The job of "rehydrating" just about can't be done without (a) a teacher or (b) a good commentary. (Usually the teacher uses the commentary.) In these translations we will usually do this step for you, letting you struggle with the logic, values and applications and not the actual meaning of the words.

4. A Talmudic Discussion Always Starts with Two Questions

The Chain of the Tradition

The rabbis called it *"Shalshelet ha-Kabbalah,"* the Chain of the Transmission of the Tradition, but we can think of it as a game of "Telephone." In England they call it "Chinese Whispers."

In *Pirkei Avot* it is described this way:

> **Mishnah:** **Moses received Torah at Sinai and passed it on to Joshua. Joshua handed it down to the elders, the elders handed to the prophets, and the prophets handed to the Men of the Great Assembly.** Avot 1.1

But think of it like this:

Moses stands on his tiptoes on a rock on the top of Mt. Sinai. God whispers the whole Torah in his ear. Moses in turn whispers it to Joshua, who whispers it to several other elders. The telephone chain moves down Mt. Sinai, across the Wilderness and into the Land of Israel. It keeps forking like a railroad yard as teachers gain students and those students in turn gain students. It stretches for more than three thousand years as the Torah is passed from heart to heart, mouth to ear, teacher to student.

That is the essence of ORAL Torah.

It comes with a single important question: "Who you gonna trust more to get the message right, the first guy in line, or someone a thousand people later?"

That question leads the rabbis to a basic understanding that the earlier the source, the more authority it has. That in turn creates the next chart: THE LAYERS of the LAW.

Torah

Rest of the Bible

Stuff by the Tanna'im

Stuff by the Amora'im

Stuff After the Talmud Was Finished

The closer to the top, the more authority your stuff has.

Question 1

That is why the first question asked about most **Mishnayot** in the **Gemara** is just about always "Ya got a source for that?"

This question comes with one of two answers.

a. This is **d'Oraita**, which means it comes from the **Torah**, though there may be a big discussion about what verse it is based on—and different rabbis may have different theories. (Telephone! Remember?)

b. This is **d'Rabbanan**, which means that this is a law that the rabbis added because they thought that the Torah needed it. Usually these laws are **siyyag la-Torah**, "fences around the Torah." These are laws that protect Torah laws the way a fence protects a garden—if you can't get close, you can't do damage.

   A **d'Oraita** law is "no work on Shabbat." A **d'Rabbanan** law is "no touching tools on Shabbat." If I can't pick up a hammer, I can't nail in a nail.

In the Gemara, if they find an argument between two **d'Oraita** laws, that is a big problem, because we don't know what God wants from us. If we find an argument between two **d'Rabbanan** laws, that is easier to live with, because people have different opinions. But what the Gemara really likes to do is to show that each opinion actually applies to a different situation.

The secret here is that only **Tanna'im** were allowed to create **d'Rabbanan** laws. After the Mishnah was finished, rabbis were only allowed to interpret. They were no longer close enough to the top of Sinai. One way of understanding Conservative Judaism is that it allows the leading rabbis of today **d'Rabbanan** authority.

Question 2

The second question, and the one that occupies much of most Talmudic discussions, is: "Does anyone know any contradictions?"

Now that we know the source of a rule, the next issue is "Was this piece of Torah corrupted in its transmission? Did the 'telephone' game garble it?" We have no way of going back to God and checking out the original message, so we do the next best thing. We compare the new message to all the other messages we have ever received.

- If it contradicts another message, then there is probably something wrong with this message or that message.

- If it is consistent with all the other laws we have learned, if there are no contradictions, then it is probably a good transmission.

Once a teaching has been presented, the **Amora'im** ask (often off-camera) "Does anyone know any contradictions?" They then begin to use **associative logic**, searching all the laws they know that might not be consistent with the new law. Here is where the **beraitot** come into play. More often than not, the extra information in these longer and more difficult versions contains the stuff that needs to be evaluated.

The rabbis then work hard to resolve all contradictions and sort out problems in the Oral Torah they received from their teachers. This does not always work.

Often a **sugia**, a Talmudic conversation, is made up of the resolution of a string of possible contradictions, one after the other.

Epilogue: Using This Translation

Talmud with Training Wheels utilizes a unique translation of the Talmudic text that has been carefully engineered to make it easier for beginners to follow the thread of the argument. More than ten years of experimentation in ongoing adult classes has gone into this process.

The Sugia

Even though the Talmud is accessed by page (a or b), it is organized by **sugia**. A **sugia** is a conversation. It is made up of a passage (usually one law) from the **Mishnah** and then all of the discussion by the **Amora'im** of that **Mishnah**. When the **Gemara** quotes another **Mishnah**, the next **sugia** begins.

Think of a **sugia** as taking place in the middle of a high-tech studio complex with a huge reference library of sound bites and film clips that each of the participants can use to clarify the text and "prove" his point of view. (There are very few *hers* in the Talmud.) A **sugia** is one discussion of the text's meaning that makes use of lots of earlier discussions. To make matters confusing, this final discussion (made up of lots of earlier pieces) has often been edited and cleaned up.

Talmud takes place in the world's best high-tech studio—the mind.

To help you decode this process, we have done five things:

1. Our Translations Look Like Scripts

Because the Talmud grew out of conversations, we have done the best we can to reconstruct those conversations. In the yeshiva, students often sing those conversations back to life. We have used formatting to help that process. Despite the look of the page, the translation is the real text, not a paraphrase or modification.

2. Our Scripts Use a Number of Typefaces

To help you keep track of the layers of the Talmud, we use different typefaces to help you understand what you are reading.

Torah: Anything that comes from the Bible shows up in this typeface. We call pieces from the Prophets and Writings Torah, because they are part of the "Torah she-b'Khtav," the "Written Law."

Tanna'im: Anything that comes from the era of the Mishnah, a piece of Mishnah or a Baraita is in this typeface.

Amora'im: Texts from the era of the Gemara, anything that isn't quoted from a Tanna'itic or biblical source, show up in this typeface.

Commentators: Any teachers who have added their interpretations to the Talmud (that we have chosen to include) are presented in this typeface. Rather than including them as footnotes. we have made them part of the dialogue. adding their voices to the conversation.

Gris: Anything that has been added by your author will be added in this typeface.

3. We Insert Biographies of Each of the Voices

These will allow you not only to grow familiar with individual Talmudic teachers but to gain a sense of the relationship between the speakers and to have an idea of what conversations were in "real time" and which were "reconstructed."

4. The Translations Are Idiomatic

This translation is not concerned with accurately reproducing every word of the Talmud in English; rather, it is a phrase-for-phrase translation, allowing you to enter easily into the conversation.

5. Notes and Reference Material

Introductions, notes and additional resources are added to the text in the margins to make the passage easy to follow. These will help to explain, explicate and contextualize the passages we are studying.

Lexicon of Talmudic Vocabulary

Often, especially when you are starting, studying Talmud feels like you are learning a second language. Here are all the important terms used in the booklet. These are the ones you really need to remember.

Amora'im: The *Amora'im* is the name given to the rabbis who wrote the Gemara. One is called an *Amora*. They lived and worked between about 200 and 500 C.E. The name means "speaker" because they were the ones who "said" the Oral Tradition.

Amud: *Amud* is the name give to a single side of a Talmudic page. A single sheet of paper, a *Daf,* is broken into *Amud a* and *Amud b*. *Amud* comes from a Hebrew word that means *pillar* or *column*. An Amud is a *column* of text.

Baraita: A *Baraita* is the technical term for teachings from the *Tanna'im*, those who wrote the Mishnah, that were not collected in the Mishnah. The Gemara frequently quotes *Beraitot* passages and uses them interchangeably with (and with the same authority as) *Mishnayot*.

Daf: A *Daf* is a Talmudic page. It is both sides of that page.

d'Oraita: *D'Oraita* is Aramaic for "from the Bible." This is the technical term for a law or teaching that comes directly from God because it can be rooted in a verse from the Torah.

d'Rabbanan: *D'Rabbanan* means "from the rabbis." This is a law or teaching that one (or more) of the *Tanna'im* (rabbis of the Mishnah) added to the Jewish tradition. Most of these laws are "fences" to protect the Torah.

Gemara: The *Gemara* is the name for the second layer of the Talmud, the one added to the *Mishnah* by the *Amora'im*. When we say the *Gemara,* we are usually also talking about the *Mishnah*, because *Gemara* is often another word for Talmud. When we say *Gemara* we are almost always talking about the Babylonian Talmud. The Jerusalem Talmud is a different story.

Masekhet/Tractate: *Masekhet* is Hebrew. *Tractate* is the English word. Both of them refer to a section of the *Mishnah* or a volume of the Talmud that is a collection of material organized around a single topic.

Midrash: The *Midrash* is made up of a number of collections of material, written by the same rabbis who wrote the Talmud, that struggle with and express the meaning of the biblical text. For the most part, Talmud involves itself with the ways that we live the Torah. For the most part, *Midrash* concerns itself with the meaning of the biblical text.

Mishnah: The *Mishnah* is the first layer of the Talmud. It was written by the *Tanna'im* in *Eretz Yisrael* between 160 B.C.E. and 210 C.E. The *Mishnah* is primarily a law code, a collection of rules that adapts the Torah to living in the modern times of the Greco-Roman Era. The *Mishnah* is divided into six orders, or *Sedarim*.

Rashi: Rashi is an acronym for Rabbi Shlomo Yitzhaki. He is "the Jewish Commentator" on both the Talmud and the Bible. For the most part, his work forms the central path that Jews use to study these texts. Rashi lived in France before and during the first Crusade.

Seder: *Seder* means order. It is the name of six organizing divisions of the *Mishnah*—and, therefore, of the entire Talmud. The name **Shas** is an abbreviation of *Shishah Sedarim*, the six orders. *Shas* is a name often used for a complete set of the volumes in the Talmud.

Sugia: A Talmudic conversation is called a *sugia*. A *sugia* is made up of a piece of *Mishnah*, usually one "law," and all of the discussion in the *Gemara* that follows from it. A *sugia* is the basic unit for Talmudic study.

Tanna'im: The rabbis who wrote the *Mishnah* are called the *Tanna'im*. One such rabbi is called a *Tanna*. These rabbis worked in *Eretz Yisrael* between about 160 B.C.E. and 210 C.E.

Torah she-b'Al Peh: *Torah she-b'Al Peh* is the Hebrew term for the "Oral Torah" or the "Oral Law." This term means two different things. First, it refers to all literature based on the Torah that comes after the Torah, including Talmud, Midrash and later Codes and Commentaries. Its other meaning is the process of extracting meaning from the Torah through a process of constant unfolding of the text.

Torah she-b'Khtav: This is the term for the "Written Torah." This is the actual collection of words that were revealed to people by God. It is the text of the Bible, the Torah, the Prophets and the Writings.

Tosafot: These were Rashi's descendents and students who wrote commentaries on Rashi's commentary. On a page of the Talmud, Rashi's commentary runs along one side and the commentary by the *Tosafot* runs down the other.

My first Talmud teacher was a saintly Holocaust survivor named Avraham. He began our first lesson with this simple statement: "Friends, today I am going to throw you into the Sea of Talmud. But don't be afraid. I am standing here on the shore ready to save you."

I hope to do the same for you. I was an adult who was thrown without knowing how to swim into the Sea of Talmud. It was very frustrating. I nearly drowned many times—and with long and patient explanations he revived me. For Jews, mouth-to-mouth resuscitation is called "*Torah she-b'Al Peh*"—the Oral transmission of the law and tradition—because it is in the teaching and the learning that we and the text are renewed.

I have a towel and an oversized shepherd's crook standing by.

Joel Lurie Grishaver